THE GARDEN OF BRIGHT WATERS;
ONE HUNDRED AND TWENTY ASIATIC LOVE POEMS

By

EDWARD POWYS MATHERS

The Garden Of Bright Waters;
One Hundred and Twenty Asiatic Love Poems
by **Edward Powys Mathers**

ISBN: 978-93-57488-56-3

Published by

DOUBLE 9 BOOKS

2/13-B, Ansari Road, Daryaganj
New Delhi – 110002
info@double9books.com
www.double9books.com
Tel. 011-40042856

ABOUT THE AUTHOR

Edward Powys Mathers, a British poet, editor, and translator, lived from 1892 until 1939. He was born in Forest Hill, London, and went to Oxford University to study contemporary languages. In particular, Japanese haiku and Chinese poetry piqued Mathers' interest in Asian poetry and literature. He translated the writings of Asian poets including Li Po, Tu Fu, and Basho and produced numerous volumes of his own poetry. Mathers' contributions to Asian poetry and his support of modernist literature in Britain are what will remain of him. Readers and academics all across the globe continue to study and enjoy his poems and translations.

CONTENTS

INTRODUCTION 7

AFGHANISTAN 8

ANNAM...21

ARABIC...26

BALUCHISTAN...39

BURMA 40

CAMBODIA...41

CAUCASUS 42

CHINA...46

DAGHESTAN..55

GEORGIA..56

HINDUSTAN 57

JAPAN 59

KAFIRISTAN 63

KAZACKS..65

KOREA 67

KURDISTAN 69

LAOS..71

MANCHURIA..74

PERSIA 75

SIAM 78

SYRIA...79

TATARS..80

THIBET 81

TURKESTAN 82

TURKEY 84

TRANSLATOR'S NOTES 86

INTRODUCTION

Head in hand, I look at the paper leaf;
It is still white.

I look at the ink
Dry on the end of my brush.

My soul sleeps.
Will it ever wake?   .

I walk a little in the pouring of the sun
And pass my hands over the higher flowers.

There is the soft green forest,
There are the sweet lines of the mountains
Carved with snow, red in the sunlight.

I see the slow march of the clouds,
I hear the crows jeering, and I come back

To sit and look at the paper leaf,
Which is still white
Under my brush.

From the Chinese of Chang-Chi (770-850).

AFGHANISTAN

THE PRINCESS OF QULZUM

(BALLADE BY NUR UDDIN)

I have seen a small proud face brimming with sunlight;
I have seen the daughter of the King of Qulzum passing from grace to grace.
Yesterday she threw her bed on the floor of her double house
And laughed with a thousand graces.
She has a little pearl and coral cap
And rides in a palanquin with servants about her
And claps her hands, being too proud to call.
I have seen a small proud face brimming with sunlight.

"My palanquin is truly green and blue;
I fill the world with pomp and take my pleasure;
I make men run up and down before me,
And am not as young a girl as you pretend.
I am of Iran, of a powerful house, I am pure steel.
I hear that I am spoken of in Lahore."
I have seen a small proud face brimming with sunlight.

I also hear that they speak of you in Lahore,
You walk with a joyous step,
Your nails are red and the palms of your hands are rosy.
A pear-tree with a fresh stem is in your palace gardens,

I would not that your mother should give my pear-tree
To twine with an evil spice-tree or fool banana.
I have seen a small proud face brimming with sunlight.

"The coins that my father gave me for my forehead
Throw rays and light the hearts of far men;
The ray of light from my red ring is sharper than a diamond.
I go about and about in pride as of hemp wine
And my words are chosen.
But I give you my honey cheeks, dear, I trust them to you."
I have seen a small proud face brimming with sunlight.

The words of my mouth are coloured and shining things;
And two great saints are my perpetual guards.
There is never a song of
Nur Uddin
but has in it a great achievement
And is as brilliant as a young hyacinth;
I pour a ray of honey on my disciples,
There is as it were a fire in my ballades.
I have seen a small proud face brimming with sunlight.
From the Pus'hto (Afghans, nineteenth century).

COME, MY BELOVED!

Come, my beloved! And I say again: Come, my beloved!
The doves are moaning and calling and will not cease.
  Come, my beloved!

"The fairies have made me queen, and my heart is love.
Sweeter than the green cane is my red mouth."
  Come, my beloved!

The jacinth has spilled odour on your hair,
The balance of your neck is like a jacinth;
You have set a star of green between your brows.
  Come, my beloved!

Like lemon-trees among the rocks of grey hills
Are the soft colours of the airy veil
To your rose knee from your curved almond waist.
  Come, my beloved!

Your light breast veil is tawny brown with stags,
Stags with eyes of emerald, hunted by red kings.
  Come, my beloved!

Muhammad Din is wandering; he is drunken and mad;
For a year he has been dying. Send for the doctor!
  Come, my beloved!
From the Pus›hto of Muhammad Din Tilai (Afghans, nineteenth century).

BALLADE OF MUHAMMAD KHAN

She has put on her green robe, she has put on her double veil, my idol;
My idol has come to me.
She has put on her green robe, my love is a laughing flower;
Gently, gently she comes, she is a young rose, she has come out of the garden.

Gently she has shown her face, parting her veil, my idol;
My idol has come to me.
She has put on her green robe, my love is a young rose for me to break.
Her chin has the smooth colour of peaches and she guards it well;
She is the daughter of a Moghol house and well they guard her.

She put on her red jewels when she came with a noise of rings, my idol;

My idol has come to me.
She has put on her green robe, my love is the stem of a rose;
She breaks not, she is strong.
She has a throne, but comes into the woods for love.

I was well and she troubled me when she came to me in the evening, my idol;
My idol has come to me.
She has put on her green robe, her wrist is a sword.
The villages speak of her; the child is as fair as Badri.
She has red lips and six hundred and fifty beads upon her light blue scarf.
Give your garland to *Muhammad Khan* , my idol;
My idol has come to me.

From the Pus'hto (Afghans, nineteenth century).

GHAZAL OF TAVAKKUL

To-day I saw Laila's breasts, the hills of a fair city
From which my heart might leap to heaven.

Her breasts are a garden of white roses
Having two drifted hills of fallen rose-leaves.

Her breasts are a garden where doves are singing
And doves are moaning with arrows because of her.

All her body is a flower and her face is Shalibagh ;
She has fruits of beautiful colours and the doves abide there.

Over the garden of her breasts she combs the gold rain of her hair....
You have killed *Tavakkul* , the faithful pupil of Abdel Qadir Gilani

From the Pus'hto (Afghans, nineteenth century).

GHAZAL OF SAYYID KAMAL

I am burning, I am crumbled into powder,
I stand to the lips in a tossing sea of tears.

Like a stone falling in Hamun lake I vanish;
I return no more, I am counted among the dead.

I am consumed like yellow straw on red flames;
You have drawn a poisoned sword along my throat to-day.

People have come to see me from far towns,
Great and small, arriving with bare heads,
For I have become one of the great historical lovers.

In the desire of your red lips
My heart has become a red kiln, like a terrace of roses.
It is because she does not trouble about the bee on the rose
That my heart is taken.

"I have blackened my eyes to kill you, *Sayyid Kamal*
I kill you with my eyelids; I am Natarsa, the Panjabie, the pitiless."

From the Pus'hto (Afghans, nineteenth century).

GHAZAL OF SAYYID AHMAD

My heart is torn by the tyranny of women very quietly;
Day and night my tears are wearing away my cheeks very quietly.

Life is a red thing like the sun setting very quietly;
Setting quickly and heavily and very quietly.

If you are to buy heaven by a good deed, to-day the market is open;
To-morrow is a day when no man buys,
And the caravan is broken up very quietly.

The kings are laughing and the slaves are laughing; but for your sake
Sayyid Ahmad is walking and mourning very quietly.

From the Pus'hto (Afghans, nineteenth century).

GHAZAL, IN LAMENT FOR THE DEAD, OF PIR MUHAMMAD

The season of parting has come up with the wind;
My girl has hollowed my heart with the hot iron of separation.

Keep away, doctor, your roots and your knives are useless.
None ever cured the ills of the ill of separation.

There is no one near me noble enough to be told;
I tear my collar in the "Alas! Alas!" of separation.

She was a branch of santal; she closed her eyes and left me.
Autumn has come and she has gone, broken to pieces in the wind of
separation.

I am *Pir Muhammad* and I am stumbling away to die;
She stamped on my eyes with the foot of separation.

From the Pus'hto (Afghans, nineteenth century).

BALLADE OF NURSHALI

Come in haste this dusk, dear child. I will be on the water path
When your girl friends go laughing by the road.
"Come in haste this dusk; I have become your nightingale,
And the young girls leave me alone because of you.
I give you the poppy of my mouth and my fallen hair."
Come in haste this dusk, dear child.

"I have dishevelled and spread out my hair for you;
Take my wrist, for there is no shame
And my father has gone out.
Sit near me on this red bed quietly."
  Come in haste this dusk, dear child.

"Sit near me on this red bed, I lift the poppy to your lips;
Your hand is strong upon my breast;
My beauty is a garden and you the bird in the flowering tree."
  Come in haste this dusk, dear child.

"My beauty is a garden with crimson flowers."
But I cannot reach over the thicket of your hair.
This is *Nurshali*
sighing for the garden;
  Come in haste this dusk, dear child.
  From the Pus›hto (Afghans).

GHAZAL OF MUHAMMAD DIN TILAI

The world is fainting,
And you will weep at last.

The world is fainting
And falling into a swoon.

The world is turning and changing;
The world is fainting,
And you will weep at last.

Look at the love of Farhad, who pierced a mountain
And pierced a brass hill for the love of Shirin.
The world is fainting,
And you will weep at last.

Qutab Khan of the Ranizais was in love
And death became the hostess of his lady.
The world is fainting,
And you will weep at last.

Adam loved Durkho, and they were separated.
You know the story;
There is no lasting love.
The world is fainting,
And you will weep at last.

Muhammad Din is ill for the matter of a little honey;
This is a moment to be generous.
The world is fainting,
And you will weep at last.

From the Pus'hto (Afghans, nineteenth century).

MICRA

When you lie with me and love me,
You give me a second life of young gold;
And when you lie with me and love me not,
I am as one who puts out hands in the dark
And touches cold wet death.

From the Pus'hto of Mirza Rahchan Kayil (Afghans, nineteenth century).

BALLADE OF MUHAMMAD DIN TILAI

A twist of fresh flowers on your dark hair,
And your hair is a panther's shadow.
On your white cheeks the down of a thousand roses,
They speak about your beauty in Lahore.
You have your mother's lips;

Your ring is frosted with rubies,
And your hair is a panther's shadow.

Your ring is frosted with rubies;
I was unhappy and you looked over the wall,
I saw your face among the crimson lilies;
There is no armour that a lover can buy,
And your hair is a panther's shadow.

"The cool fingers of the mistress burn her lovers
And they go away.
I have fatigued the wise of many lands,
And my hair is a tangle of serpents.
What is the profit of these shawls without you?
And my hair is a panther's shadow."

"A squadron of my father's men are about me,
And I have woven a collar of yellow flowers.
My eyes are veiled because I drink cups of bhang,
Being a daughter of the daughter of queens.
You cannot touch me because of my palaces,
And my hair is a panther's shadow."

I will touch you, though your beauty be as fair as song;
For I am a disciple ofAbdel Qadir Gilani ,
And my songs are as beautiful as women and as strong as love;
And your hair is a panther's shadow.

Your ring is frosted with rubies....
Muhammad Din awaits the parting of your scarves;
Tilai is standing here, young and magnificent like a tree;
And your hair is a panther's shadow.
From the Pus'hto (Afghans, nineteenth century).

GHAZAL OF MIRA

The lover to his lass: I have fallen before your door.
I came to ask for alms and have lost my all,
I had a copper-shod quarter-staff but the dogs attacked me,
And not a strand of her hair came the way of my lips.
The lover to his lass: I have fallen before your door.

The lamp burns and I must play the green moth.
I have stolen her scented rope of flowers,
But the women caught me and built a little gaol
About my heart with your old playthings.
The lover to his lass: I have fallen before your door.

Mira is a mountain goat that climbs to die
Upon the top peak in the rocks of grief;
It is the hour; make haste.
The lover to his lass: I have fallen before your door.
From the Pus'hto (Afghans, nineteenth century).

GHAZAL OF MAJID SHAH

Grief is hard upon me, Master, for she has left me;
The black dust has covered my pretty one.

My heart is black, for the tomb has taken my friend;
How pleasantly would go the days if my friend were here.

I can only dream of the stature of my friend;
The flowers are dying in my heart, my breast is a fading garden.

Her breast is a sweet garden now, and her garments are gold flowers;
I am an orchard at night, for my friend has gone a journey.

I am*Majid Shah* , a slave that ministers to the dead;Abdel Qadir Gilani,
even the Master, shall not save me.

From the Pus'hto (Afghans, nineteenth century).

GHAZAL OF MIRA

The world passes, nothing lasts, and the creation of men
Is buried alive under the vault of Time.

Autumn comes pillaging gardens;
The bulbuls laugh to see the flowers falling.

Wars start up wherever your eye glances,
And the young men moan marching on to the batteries.

Mira is the unkempt old man you see on the road;
He has taken his death-wound in battle.
From the Pus'hto (Afghans, nineteenth century).

BALLADE OF AJAM THE WASHERMAN

Come to me to-day wearing your green collar,
Make your two orange sleeves float in the air, and come to me.
Touch your hair with essence and colour your clothes yellow;
The deer of reason has fled from the hill of my heart;
Come to me.

The deer of reason has fled from the hill of my heart
Because I have seen your gold rings and your amber rings;
Your eyes have lighted a small fire below my heart,

Put on your gold rings and your amber rings, and come to me.
Put on your gold rings and your amber rings, and you will be more beautiful
Than the brown girls of poets and the milk-white wives of kings.
The coil of your hair is like a hangman's rope;
But press me to your green collar between your orange sleeves.

Press me to your green collar between your orange sleeves,
And give yourself once to *Ajam*. Slip away weeping,
Slip weeping away from the house of the wicked, and come to me.
Come to me to-day wearing your green collar,
Make your two orange sleeves float in the air and come to me.

From the Pus'hto (Afghans).

GHAZAL OF ISA AKHUN ZADA

Beauty with the flame shawl, do not repulse me;
Breathing idol of rose ivory, look at me;
Beauty with the flame shawl, let me say a little thing,
Lend your small ears to my quick sighing.
Breathing idol, I have come to the walls of death;
And there are coloured cures behind the crystal of your eyes.
Life is a tale ill constructed without love.
Beauty of the flame shawl, do not repulse me;
I am at your door wasted and white and dying.
Breathing idol of rose ivory, look at me;
Beauty with the flame shawl, do not repulse me.

This is the salaam that slaves make, and after the salaam
Listen to these quick sighings and their wisdom.
All the world has spied on us and seen our love,
And in four days or five days will be whispering evil.
Knot your robes in a turban, escape and be mine for ever;
Beauty with the flame shawl, do not repulse me.
After that we will both of us go to prison.
Breathing idol of rose ivory, look at me;
Beauty with the flame shawl, do not repulse me.

My quick sighings carry a tender promise;
I will have time to remember in the battle,

Though all the world is a thousand whistling swords against me.
The iron is still in the rock that shall forge my death-sword,
Though I have foes more than the stars
Of a thousand valley starlights.
Breathing idol of rose ivory, look at me;
Beauty with the flame shawl, do not repulse me.

I am as strong as Sikander , I am as strong as death;
You will hear me come with guns brooding behind me,
And laughing bloody battalions following after.
Isa Gal
is stronger than God;
Do not whip me, do not whip me,
Beauty with the flame shawl, do not repulse me;
Breathing idol of rose ivory, look at me.
Breathing idol of rose ivory, look at me;
Beauty with the flame shawl, do not repulse me.
From the Pus'hto (Afghans, nineteenth century).

ANNAM

THE BAMBOO GARDEN

Old bamboos are about my house,
And the floor of my house is untidy with old books.
It is sweet to rest in the shade of it
And read the poems of the masters.

But I remember a delightful fisherman
Who played on the five-stringed dan in the evening.
In the day he allowed his reed canoe to float
Over the lakes and rivers,
Watching his nets and singing.

A sweet boy promised to marry me,
But he went away and left
Like a reed canoe that rolls adrift
In the middle of a river.
Song of Annam.

STRANGER THINGS HAVE HAPPENED

Do not believe that ink is always black,
   Or lime white, or lemon sour;
You cannot ring one bell from two pagodas,
You cannot have two governors for the city of Lang Son.
   I found you binding an orange spray
   Of flowers with white flowers;

I never noticed the flower gathering
Of other village ladies.
Would you like me to go and see your father and mother?

Song of Annam.

NOCTURNE

It is late at night
And the North Star is shining.
The mist covers the rice-fields
And the bamboos
Are whispering full of crickets.
The watch beats on the iron-wood gong,
And priests are ringing the pagoda bells.
We hear the far-away games of peasants
And distant singing in the cottages.

It is late at night.
As we talk gently,
Sitting by one another,
Life is as beautiful as night.
The red moon is rising
On the mountain side
Like a fire started among the trees.
There is the North Star
Shining like a paper lantern.
The light air brings dew to our faces
And the sound of tamtams beaten far away.
Let us sit like this all night.

Song of Annam.

THE GAO FLOWER

I am the Gao flower high in a tree,

You are the grass Long Mai on the path-side.
When heat comes down after the dews of morning
The flower grows pale and tumbles on the grass,
The grass Long Mai that keeps the fallen Gao.

Folk who let their daughters grow
Without achieving a husband
Might easily forget to fence their garden,
Or let their radishes grow flower and rank
When they could eat them ripe and tender.

Come to me, you that I see walk
Every night in a red turban;
Young man with the white turban, come to me.
We will plant marrows together in a garden,
And there may be little marrows for your children.

I will dye your turban blue and red and yellow,
You with the white turban.
You that are passing with a load of water,
I call you
And you do not even turn your head.

Song of Annam.

THE GIRL OF KE-MO

I'm a girl of Ke-Mo village
Selling my rice wine on the road.
Mine is the strongest rice wine in the land,
Though my bottle is so patched and dirty.
These silly rags are not my body,
The parts you cannot see are counted pleasant;
But you are just too drunk to drink my wine,
And just too plain to lie down on my mat.

He who would drink the wine of the girl of Ke-Mo
Needs a beautiful body and a lofty wit.

Song of Annam.

THE LITTLE WOMAN OF CLEAR RIVER

Clear River twists nine times about
Clear River; but so deep
That none can see the green sand.
You hear the birds about Clear River:
Dik, dik, dik, dik, Diu dik.

A little woman with jade eyes
Leans on the wall of a pavilion.
She has the moonrise in her heart
And the singing of love songs
Comes to her up the river.

She stands and dreams for me
Outside the house by the bamboo door.
In a minute
I will leave my shadow
And talk to her of poetry and love.

Song of Annam.

WAITING TO MARRY A STUDENT

I still walk slowly on the river bank
Where I came singing,
And where I saw your boat pass up beyond the sun
Setting red in the river.
I want Autumn,
I want the leaves to begin falling at once,
So that the cold time may bring us close again
LikeK'ien Niü andChik Nü, the two stars.

Each year when Autumn comes
The crows make a black bridge across the milky sea,
And then these two poor stars
Can run together in gold and be at peace.
Darling, for my sake work hard
And be received with honour at the Examinations.

Since I saw your boat pass up beyond the sun
I have forgotten how to sing
And how to paddle the canoe across the lake.
I know how to sit down and how to be sad,
And I know how to say nothing;
But every other art has slipped away.

Song of Annam.

A SONG FOR TWO

I have lacquered my teeth to find a husband.

And I have need of a wife.
Give me a kiss and they will marry us
At Mo-Lao, my village.

I will marry you if you will wait for me,
Wait till the banana puts forth branches,
And fruit hangs heavy on the Sung-tree,
And the onion flowers;
Wait till the dove goes down in the pool to lay her eggs,
And the eel climbs into a tree to make her nest.

Song of Annam.

ARABIC

SAND

The sand is like acres of wet milk
Poured out under the moonlight;
It crawls up about your brown feet
Like wine trodden from white stars.

From the Arabic of John Duncan .

TWO SIMILES

You have taken away my cloak,
My cloak of weariness;
Take my coat also,
My many-coloured coat of life....

On this great nursery floor
I had three toys,
A bright and varnished vow,
A Speckled Monster, best of boys,
True friend to me, and more
Beloved and a thing of cost,
My doll painted like life; and now
One is broken and two are lost.

From the Arabic of John Duncan .

MELODIAN

I have been at this shooting-gallery too long.
It is monotonous how the little coloured balls
Make up and down on their silvery water thread;
It would be pleasant to have money and go instead
To watch your greasy audience in the threepenny stalls
Of the World-famous Caravan of Dance and Song.

And I want to go out beyond the turf fires there,
After I've looked at your just smiling face,
To that untented silent dark blue nighted place;
And wait such time as you will wish the noise all dumb
And drop your fairings and leave the funny man, and come ...
You have the most understanding face in all the fair.

From the Arabic of John Duncan .

THE LOST LADY

You are the drowned,
Star that I found
Washed on the rim of the sea
Before the morning.
You are the little dying light
That stopped me in the night.

From the Arabic of John Duncan .

LOVE BROWN AND BITTER

You know so well how to stay me with vapours
Distilled expertly to that unworthy end;
You know the poses of your body I love best
And that I am cheerful with your head on my breast,

You know you please me by disliking one friend;
You read up what amuses me in the papers.

Who knows me knows I am not of those fools
That gets tired of a woman who is kind to them,
Yet you know not how stifled you render me
By learning me so well, how I long to see
An unpractised girl under your clever phlegm,
A soul not so letter-perfect in the rules.

From the Arabic of John Duncan .

OKHOUAN

A mole shows black
Between her mouth and cheek.

As if a negro,
Coming into a garden,
Wavered between a purple rose
And a scarlet camomile.

From the Arabic.

LYING DOWN ALONE

I shall never see your tired sleep
In the bed that you make beautiful,
Nor hardly ever be a dream
That plays by your dark hair;
Yet I think I know your turning sigh
And your trusting arm's abandonment,
For they are the picture of my night,
My night that does not end.

From the Arabic of John Duncan .

OLD GREEK LOVERS

They put wild olive and acanthus up
With tufts of yellow wool above the door
When a man died in Greece and in Greek Islands,
   Grey stone by the blue sea,
Or sage-green trees down to the water's edge.
   How many clanging years ago
  I, also withering into death, sat with him,
   Old man of so white hair who only,
   Only looked past me into the red fire.
At last his words were all a jumble of plum-trees
And white boys smelling of the sea's green wine
And practice of his lyre. Suddenly
   The bleak resurgent mind
Called wonderfully clear: "What mark have I left?"
  Crying girls with wine and linen
Washed the straight old body and wrapped up,
   And set the doorward feet.
Later for me also under Greek sun
The pendant leaves in green and bitter flakes
Blew out to join the wastage of the world,
And wool, I take it, in the nests of birds.

From the Arabic of John Duncan .

NIGHT AND MORNING

The great brightness of the burning of the stars,
Little frightened love,
Is like your eyes,
When in the heavy dusk
You question the dark blue shadows,
Fearing an evil.

Below the night

The one clear line of dawn;
As it were your head
Where there is one golden hair
Though your hair is very brown.

From the Arabic (School of Ebn-el-Moattaz) (ninth century).

IN A YELLOW FRAME

Her hand tinted to gold with henna
Gave me a cup of wine like gold water,
And I said: The moon rise, the sun rise.

From the Arabic of Hefny-bey-Nassif (contemporary).

BECAUSE THE GOOD ARE NEVER FAIR

When she appears the daylight envies her garment,
The wanton daylight envies her garment
To show it to the jealous sun.

And when she walks,
All women tall and tiny
Want her figure and start crying.

Because of your mouth,
Long life to the Agata valley,
Long life to pearls.

Watchers have discovered paradise in your cheeks,
But I am undecided,
For there is a hint of the tops of flames
In their purple shining.

From the Arabic of Ahmed Bey Chawky (contemporary).

WHITE AND GREEN AND BLACK TEARS

Why are your tears so white?

Dear, I have wept so long
That my old tears grow white like my old hair.

Why are your tears so green?

Dear, the waters are wept away
And the green gall is flowing.

Why are your tears so black?

Dear, the weeping is over
And the black flash you loved is breaking.

From the Arabic (School of Ebn-el-Farid) (thirteenth century).

A CONCEIT

I hide my love,
I will not say her name.
And yet since I confess
I love, her name is told.
You know that if I love
It must be ... Whom?

From the Arabic of Ebn Kalakis Abu El Fath Nasrallah (eleventh century).

VALUES

Since there is excitement
In suffering for a woman,
Let him burn on.
The dust in a wolf's eyes
Is balm of flowers to the wolf
When a flock of sheep has raised it.

From the Arabic.

WHAT LOVE IS

Love starts with a little throb in the heart,

And in the end one dies
Like an ill-treated toy.
Love is born in a look or in four words,
The little spark that burnt the whole house.
Love is at first a look,
And then a smile,
And then a word,
And then a promise,
And then a meeting of two among flowers.

From the Arabic.

THE DANCING HEART

When she came she said:
You know that your love is granted,
Why is your heart trembling?

And I:

You are bringing joy for my heart
And so my heart is dancing.

From the Arabic of Urak El Hutail.

THE GREAT OFFENCE

She seemed so bored,
I wanted to embrace her by surprise;
But then the scalding waters
Fell from her eyes and burnt her roses.

I offered her a cup....

And came to paradise....

Ah, sorrow,
When she rose from the waves of wine
I thought she would have killed me

With the swords of her desolation....

Especially as I had tied her girdle
With the wrong bow.

From the Arabic of Abu Nuas (eighth century).

AN ESCAPE

She was beautiful that evening and so gay....

In little games
My hand had slipped her mantle,
I am not sure
About her skirts.

Then in the night's curtain of shadows,
Heavy and discreet,
I asked and she replied:
To-morrow.

Next day I came
Saying, Remember.

Words of a night, she said, to bring the day.

From the Arabic of Abu Nuas (eighth century).

THREE QUEENS

Three sweet drivers hold the reins,
And hold the places of my heart.
A great people obeys me,
But these three obey me not.
Am I then a lesser king than love?

From the Arabic of Haroun El Raschid (eighth century).

HER NAILS

She is as wise as Hippocrates,
As beautiful as Joseph,
As sweet-voiced as David,
As pure as Mary.

I am as sad as Jacob,
As lonely as Jonah,
As patient as Job,
As unfortunate as Adam.

When I met her again
And saw her nails
Prettily purpled,
I reproached her for making up
When I was not there.

She told me gently
That she was no coquette,
But had wept tears of blood
Because I was not there,
And maybe she had dried her eyes
With her little hands.

I would like to have wept before she wept;
But she wept first
And has the better love.
Her eyes are long eyes,
And her brows are the bows of subtle strong men.

From the Arabic of Yazid Ebn Moauia (seventh century).

PERTURBATION AT DAWN

Day comes....

And when she sees the withering of the violet garden
And the saffron garden flowering,

The stars escaping on their black horse
And dawn on her white horse arriving,
She is afraid.

Against the sighing of her frightened breasts
She puts her hand;
I see what I have never seen,
Five perfect lines on a crystal leaf
Written with coral pens.

From the Arabic of Ebn Maatuk (seventeenth century).

THE RESURRECTION OF THE TATTOOED GIRL

Her hands are filled with what I lack,
And on her arms are pictures,
Looking like files of ants forsaking the battalions,
Or hail inlaid by broken clouds on green lawns.

She fears the arrows of her proper eyes
And has her hands in armour.

She has stretched her hands in a cup to me,
Begging for my heart.
She has circled me with the black magic of her brows
And shot small arrows at me.

The black curl that lies upon her temple
Is a scorpion pointing his needle at the stars.

Her eyes seem tight, tight shut;
But I believe she is awake.

From the Arabic of Yazid Ebn Moauia (seventh century).

MOALLAKA

The poets have muddied all the little fountains.

Yet do not my strong eyes know you, far house?

O dwelling of Abla in the valley of Gawa,

Speak to me, for my camel and I salute you.

My camel is as tall as a tower, and I make him stand

And give my aching heart to the wind of the desert.

O erstwhile dwelling of Abla in the valley of Gawa;

And my tribe in the valleys of Hazn and Samna
And in the valley of Motethalem!

Salute to the old ruins, the lonely ruins

Since Oum El Aythan gathered and went away.

Now is the dwelling of Abla

In a valley of men who roar like lions.
It will be hard to come to you, O daughter of Makhram.

     *   *   *   *   *

Abla is a green rush

That feeds beside the water.

But they have taken her to Oneiza

And my tribe feeds in lazy Ghailam valley.

They fixed the going, and the camels

Waked in the night and evilly prepared.

I was afraid when I saw the camels

Standing ready among the tents
And eating grain to make them swift.

I counted forty-two milk camels,

Black as the wings of a black crow.

White and purple are the lilies of the valley,

But Abla is a branch of flowers.

Who will guide me to the dwelling of Abla?

From the Arabic of <u>Antar</u> *(late sixth and early seventh centuries).*

MOALLAKA

Rise and hold up the curved glass,
And pour us wine of the morning, of El Andar.

Pour wine for us, whose golden colour
Is like a water stream kissing flowers of saffron.

Pour us wine to make us generous
And carelessly happy in the old way.

Pour us wine that gives the miser
A sumptuous generosity and disregard.

O Oum-Amr, you have prevented me from the cup
When it should have been moving to the right;
And yet the one of us three that you would not serve
Is not the least worthy.

How many cups have I not emptied at Balbek,
And emptied at Damas and emptied at Cacerin!

More cups! more cups! for death will have his day;
His are we and he ours.

    *   *   *   *   *

By herself she is fearless
And gives her arms to the air,
The limbs of a long camel that has not borne.

She gives the air her breasts,
Unfingered ivory.

She gives the air her long self and her curved self,

And hips so round and heavy that they are tired.

All these noble abundances of girlhood
Make the doors divinely narrow and myself insane.

Columns of marble and ivory in the old way,
And anklets chinking in gold and musical bracelets.

Without her I am a she-camel that has lost,
And howls in the sand at night.

Without her I am as sad as an old mother
Hearing of the death of her many sons.

From the Arabic of Amr Ebn Kultum (seventh century).

BALUCHISTAN

COMPARISONS

Touch my hands with your fingers, yellow wallflower.
Did God use a bluer paint
Painting the sky for the gold sun
Or making the sea about your two black stars?

Treasure the touches of my fingers.

God did not spread his bluest paint
On a hollow sky or a girl's eye,
But on a topaz chain, from you to me.

Touch my temples with your fingers, scarlet rose.

Did God use a stronger light
When He fashioned and dropped the sun into the sky
Or dropped your black stars into their blue sea?

Treasure the touches of my fingers.

God did not spend His strongest light
On a sun above or a look of love,
But on a round gold ring, from you to me.

Touch my cheeks with your fingers, blue hyacinth.

Did God use a whiter silk
Weaving the veil for your fevered roses,
Or spinning the moon that lies across your face?

Treasure the touches of my fingers.

God did not waste His whitest web
On veils of silk or moons of milk,
But on a marriage cap, from you to me.

Popular Song of Baluchistan.

BURMA

A CANKER IN THE HEART

I made a bitter song
When I was a boy,
About a girl
With hot earth-coloured hair,
Who lived with me
And left me.

I made a sour song
On her marriage-day,
That ever his kisses
Would be ghosts of mine,
And ever the measure
Of his halting love
Flow to my music.

It was a silly song,
Dear wife with cool black hair,
And yet when I recall
(At night with you asleep)
That once you gave yourself
Before we met,
I do not quite well know
What song to make.

From the Burmese (nineteenth century) (¿ by Asmapur).

CAMBODIA

DISQUIET

Brother, my thought of you
In this letter on a palm-leaf
Goes up about you
As her own scent
Goes up about the rose.

The bracelets on my arms
Have grown too large
Because you went away.

I think the sun of love
Melted the snow of parting,
For the white river of tears has overflowed.

But though I am sad
I am still beautiful,
The girl that you desired
In April.

Brother, my love for you
In this letter on a palm-leaf
Brightens about you
As her own rays
Brighten about the moon.

Love Poem of Cambodia.

CAUCASUS

VENGEANCE

Aischa was mine,
My tender cousin,
My blond lover;
And you knew our love,
Uncle without bowels,
Foul old man.

For a few weights of gold
You sold her to the blacks,
And they will drive a stinking trade
At the dark market;
Your slender daughter,
The free child of our hills.

She will go to serve the bed
Of a fat man with no God,
A guts that cannot walk,
A belly hiding his own feet,
A rolling paunch
Between itself and love.

She was slim and quick
Like the antelope of our hills
When he comes down in the summer-time
To bathe in the pools of Tereck,
Her stainless flesh

Was all moonlight.

Her long silk hair

Was of so fine a gold
And of so honey-like a brown
That bees flew there,
And her red lips
Were flowers in sunlight.

She was fair, alas, she was fair,

So that her beauty goes
To a garden of dying flowers,
Made one with the girls that mourn
And wither for light and love
Behind the harem bars.

And you have dirty dreams

That she will be Sultane,
And you will drink and boast
And roll about,
The grinning ancestor
Of little kings.

Hugging your very wicked gold

Within a greasy belt,
You paddle exulting like a bald ape
That glories to defile,
Unmindful of two hot young streams
Of tears.

You stole this dirty gold,

For this gold means
Your daughter's freedom
And your nephew's love,
Two fresh and lovely things
Groaning within your belt.

The sunny playing of our childhood

At the green foot of Elbours,
The starry playing of our youth
Beyond the flowery fences,
These sigh their lost delights
Within your belt.

Give me the gold;

Damn you, give me the gold....
You kill my mercy
When you kill my love....
Hold up your trembling sword;
For this is death.

       *   *   *   *   *

I take the belt from the dead loins

That put away my love,
And turn my sweet white horse
After the caravan....
With dirty gold and clean steel
I'll set Aischa free.

Ballad of the Caucasus.

THE FLIGHT

Softly into the saddle
Of my black horse with white feet;
Your brothers are frowning
And grasping swords in sleep.
My rifle is as clean as moonlight,
My flints are new;
My long grey sword is sighing
In his blue sheath.
Fatima gave me my grey sword
Of Temrouk steel,

Damascened in red gold
To cut a pathway for the feet of love.

My eye is dark and keen,

My hand has never trembled on the sword.
If your brothers rise and follow
On their stormy horses,
If they stretch their hot hands
To catch you from my breast,
My rifle shall not sing to them,
My steel shall spare.
My rifle's song is for my yellow girl,
My eye is dark and keen,
I'll send my bullet to the fairest heart
That ever lady loved with in the world.

My hand upon the sword

Shall be so strong,
He'll find the little laughing place
Where you dance in my breast;
And we'll have no more of the silly world
Where our lips must lie apart.
We'll let death pour our souls
Into one cup,
And mount like joyous birds to God
With hearts on fire,
And God will mingle us into one shape
In an eternal garden of gold stars.

Love Ballad of the Caucasus.

CHINA

WE WERE TWO GREEN RUSHES

We were two green rushes by opposing banks,
  And the small stream ran between.
Not till the water beat us down
  Could we be brought together,
Not till the winter came
Could we be mingled in a frosty sleep,
  Locked down and close.

From the Chinese of J. Wing *(nineteenth century).*

SONG WRITER PAID WITH AIR

I sit on a white wood box
Smeared with the black name
Of a seller of white sugar.
The little brown table is so dirty
That if I had food
I do not think I could eat.

How can I promise violets drunken in wine

For your amusement,
How can I powder your blue cotton dress
With splinters of emerald,
How can I sing you songs of the amber pear,
Or pour for the finger-tips of your white fingers
Mingled scents in a rose agate bowl?

From the Chinese of J. Wing *(nineteenth century).*

THE BAD ROAD

I have seen a pathway shaded by green great trees,
A road bordered by thickets light with flowers.

My eyes have entered in under the green shadow,
And made a cool journey far along the road.

But I shall not take the road,
Because it does not lead to her house.

When she was born
They shut her little feet in iron boxes,
So that my beloved never walks the roads.

When she was born
They shut her heart in a box of iron,
So that my beloved shall never love me.

From the Chinese.

THE WESTERN WINDOW

At the head of a thousand roaring warriors,
With the sound of gongs,
My husband has departed
Following glory.

At first I was overjoyed
To have a young girl's liberty.

Now I look at the yellowing willow-leaves;
They were green the day he left.

I wonder if he also was glad?

From the Chinese of Wang Ch'ang Ling (eighth century).

IN LUKEWARM WEATHER

The women who were girls a long time ago
Are sitting between the flower bushes
And speaking softly together:

"They pretend that we are old and have white hair;
They say also that our faces
Are not like the spring moons.

"Perhaps it is a lie;
We cannot see ourselves.

"Who will tell us for certain
That winter is not at the other side of the mirror,
Obscuring our delights
And covering our hair with frost?"

From the Chinese of Wang Ch'ang Ling (eighth century).

WRITTEN ON WHITE FROST

The white frost covers all the arbute-trees,
Like powder on the faces of women.

Looking from window consider
That a man without women is like a flower
Naked without its leaves.

To drive away my bitterness

I write this thought with my narrowed breath
On the white frost.

From the Chinese of Wang Chi (sixth and seventh centuries).

A FLUTE OF MARVEL

Under the leaves and cool flowers

The wind brought me the sound of a flute
From far away.

I cut a branch of willow
And answered with a lazy song.

Even at night, when all slept,
The birds were listening to a conversation
In their own language.

From the Chinese of Li Po (705-763).

THE WILLOW-LEAF

I am in love with a child dreaming at the window.

Not for her elaborate house
On the banks of Yellow River;

But for a willow-leaf she has let fall
Into the water.

I am in love with the east breeze.

Not that he brings the scent of the flowering of peaches
White on Eastern Hill;

But that he has drifted the willow-leaf
Against my boat.

I am in love with the willow-leaf.

Not that he speaks of green spring
Coming to us again;

But that the dreaming girl
Pricked there a name with her embroidery needle,
And the name is mine.

From the Chinese of Chang Chiu Ling (675-740).

A POET LOOKS AT THE MOON

I hear a woman singing in my garden,
But I look at the moon in spite of her.

I have no thought of trying to find the singer

Singing in my garden;
I am looking at the moon.

And I think the moon is honouring me

With a long silver look.
I blink
As bats fly black across the ray;
But when I raise my head the silver look
Is still upon me.

The moon delights to make eyes of poets her mirror,

And poets are many as dragon scales
On the moonlit sea.

From the Chinese of Chang Jo Hsu.

WE TWO IN A PARK AT NIGHT

We have walked over the high grass under the wet trees
To the gravel path beside the lake, we two.
A noise of light-stepping shadows follows now
From the dark green mist in which we waded.

Six geese drop one by one into the shivering lake;

They say "Peeng" and then after a long time, "Peeng,"
Swimming out softly to the moon.

Three of the balancing dancing geese are dim and black,

And three are white and clear because of the moon;
In what explanatory dawn will our souls
Be seen to be the same?

From the Chinese of J. Wing *(nineteenth century).*

THE JADE STAIRCASE

The jade staircase is bright with dew.

Slowly, this long night, the queen climbs,

Letting her gauze stockings and her elaborate robe
Drag in the shining water.

Dazed with the light,

She lowers the crystal blind
Before the door of the pavilion.

It leaps down like a waterfall in sunlight.

While the tiny clashing dies down,

Sad and long dreaming,
She watches between the fragments of jade light
The shining of the autumn moon.

From the Chinese of Li Po (705-762).

THE MORNING SHOWER

The young lady shows like a thing of light
In the shadowy deeps of a fair window
Grown round with flowers.

She is naked and leans forward, and her flesh like frost

Gathers the light beyond the stone brim.

Only the hair made ready for the day

Suggests the charm of modern clothing.
Her blond eyebrows are the shape of very young moons.

The shower's bright water overflows

In a pure rain.

She lifts one arm into an urgent line,

Cooling her rose fingers
On the grey metal of the spray.

If I could choose my service, I would be the shower

Dashing over her in the sunlight.

From the Chinese of J.S. Ling (1901).

A VIRTUOUS WIFE

One moment I place your two bright pearls against my robe,
And the red silk mirrors a rose in each.

Why did I not meet you before I married?

See, there are two tears quivering at my lids;

I am giving back your pearls.

From the Chinese of Chang Chi (770-850).

WRITTEN ON A WALL IN SPRING

It rained last night,
But fair weather has come back
This morning.

The green clusters of the palm-trees

Open and begin to throw shadows.

But sorrow drifts slowly down about me.

I come and go in my room,

Heart-heavy with memories.

The neighbour green casts shadows of green

On my blind;
The moss, soaked in dew,
Takes the least print

Like delicate velvet.

I see again a gauze tunic of oranged rose
With shadowy underclothes of grenade red.

How things still live again.

I go and sit by the day balustrade

And do nothing

Except count the plains
And the mountains
And the valleys
And the rivers
That separate from my Spring.

From the Chinese (early nineteenth century).

A POET THINKS

The rain is due to fall,
The wind blows softly.

The branches of the cinnamon are moving,
The begonias stir on the green mounds.

Bright are the flying leaves,
The falling flowers are many.

The wind lifted the dry dust,
And he is lifting the wet dust;
Here and there the wind moves everything

He passes under light gauze

And touches me.

I am alone with the beating of my heart.

There are leagues of sky,

And the water is flowing very fast.
Why do the birds let their feathers
Fall among the clouds?

I would have them carry my letters,

But the sky is long.

The stream flows east

And not one wave comes back with news.

The scented magnolias are shining still,

But always a few are falling.

I close his box on my guitar of jasper

And lay aside my jade flute.

I am alone with the beating of my heart.

Stay with me to-night,

Old songs.

From the Chinese of Liu Chi (1311-1375).

IN THE COLD NIGHT

Reading in my book this cold night,
I have forgotten to go to sleep.
The perfumes have died on the gilded bed-cover;
The last smoke must have left the hearth
When I was not looking.
My beautiful friend snatches away the lamp.
Do you know what the time is?

From the Chinese of Yuan Mei (1715-1797).

DAGHESTAN

WINTER COMES

Winter scourges his horses
Through the North,
His hair is bitter snow
On the great wind.
The trees are weeping leaves
Because the nests are dead,
Because the flowers were nests of scent
And the nests had singing petals
And the flowers and nests are dead.

Your voice brings back the songs
Of every nest,
Your eyes bring back the sun
Out of the South,
Violets and roses peep
Where you have laughed the snow away
And kissed the snow away,
And in my heart there is a garden still
For the lost birds.

Song of Daghestan.

GEORGIA

PART OF A GHAZAL

Lonely rose out-splendouring legions of roses,
How could the nightingales behold you and not sing?

By Rustwell of Georgia (from the Tariel, twelfth century).

HINDUSTAN

FARD

Love brings the tiny sweat into your hair
Like stars marching in the dead of night.

From the Hindustani of Mir Taqui (eighteenth century).

INCURABLE

I desire the door-sill of my beloved
   More than a king›s house;
I desire the shadow of the wall where her beauty hides
   More than the Delhi palaces.
Why did you wait till spring;
Were not my hands already full of red-thorned roses?
   My heart is yours,
So that I know not which heart I hear sighing:
   Yaquin, Yaquin, Yaquin, foolish Yaquin.

From the Hindustani of Yaquin (eighteenth century).

A POEM

Joy fills my eyes, remembering your hair, with tears,
   And these tears roll and shine;
Into my thoughts are woven a dark night with raindrops
   And the rolling and shining of love songs.

From the Hindustani of Mir Taqui (eighteenth century).

FARD

Ever your rose face or black curls are with Shaguil;
Because your curls are night and your face is day.

From the Hindustani of Shaguil (eighteenth century).

MORTIFICATION

Now that the wind has taught your veil to show your eyes and hair,
All the world is bowing down to your dear head;
Faith has crept away to die beside the tomb of prayer,
And men are kneeling to your hair, and God is dead.

From the Hindustani of Hatifi (eighteenth century).

FARD

A love-sick heart dies when the heart is whole,
For all the heart's health is to be sick with love.

From the Hindustani of Miyan Jagnu (eighteenth century).

JAPAN

GRIEF AND THE SLEEVE

Tears in the moonlight,
You know why,
Have marred the flowers
On my rose sleeve.
Ask why.

From the Japanese of Hide-Yoshi.

DRINK SONG

The crows have wakened me
By cawing at the moon.
I pray that I shall not think of him;
I pray so intently
That he begins to fill my whole mind.
This is getting on my nerves;
I wonder if there is any of that wine left.

Japanese Street Song .

A BOAT COMES IN

Although I shall not see his face
For the low riding of the ship,
The three armorial oak-leaves on his cloak
Will be enough.
But what if I make a mistake And call to the wrong man?

Or make no sign at all,
And it is he?

Japanese Street Song .

THE OPINION OF MEN

My desires are like the white snows on Fuji
That grow but never melt.
I am becoming proud of my bad reputation;
And the more men say,
We cannot understand why she loves him,
The less I care.
I am sure that in a very short time
I shall give myself to him.

Japanese Street Song .

OLD SCENT OF THE PLUM-TREE

Remembering what passed
Under the scent of the plum-tree,
I asked the plum-tree for tidings
Of that other.
Alas ... the cold moon of spring....

From the Japanese of Fujiwara Ietaka. (1158-1237).

AN ORANGE SLEEVE

In the fifth month,
When orange-trees
Fill all the world with scent,
I think of the sleeve
Of a girl who loved me.

From the Japanese of Nari-hira.

INVITATION

The chief flower
Of the plum-tree of this isle
Opens to-night....
Come, singing to the moon,
In the third watch.

From the Japanese of a Courtesan of Nagasaki.

THE CLOCKS OF DEATH

In a life where the clocks
Are slow or fast,
It is a pleasant thing
To die together
As we are dying.

From the Japanese of the Wife of Bes-syo Ko-saburo Naga-haru, (sixteenth century).

GREEN FOOD FOR A QUEEN

I was gathering
Leaves of the
Wakana
In springtime.
Why did the snow fall
On my dress?

From the Japanese of the Mikado Ko-ko Ten-no, (ninth century).

THE CUSHION

Your arm should only be
A spring night's dream;
If I accepted it to rest my head upon
There would be rumours
And no delight.

From the Japanese of the daughter of Taira-no Tsu-gu-naka.

A SINGLE NIGHT

Was one night,
And that a night
Without much sleep,
Enough to make me love
All the life long?

From the Japanese of the wife of the Mikado Sui-toka In (twelfth century).

AT A DANCE OF GIRLS

Let the wind's breath
Blow in the glades of the clouds
Until they close;
So that the beauty of these girls
May not escape.

From the Japanese of So-dzyo Hend-zyo

.

ALONE ONE NIGHT

This night,
Long like the drooping feathers
Of the pheasant,
The chain of mountains,
Shall I sleep alone?

From the Japanese of Kaik-no Motto-no Hitomaro (seventh and eighth centuries).

KAFIRISTAN

WALKING UP A HILL AT DAWN

Here is the wind in the morning;
The kind red face of God
Is looking over the hill
We are climbing.

To-morrow we are going to marry
And work and play together,
And laugh together at things
Which would not amuse our neighbours.

Song of Kafiristan.

PROPOSAL OF MARRIAGE

Your eyes are black like water-melon pips,
Your lips are red like the red flesh of water-melons,
Your loins are smooth like smooth-rind water-melons.

You are more beautiful than my favourite among mares,
Your buttocks are sleeker and firmer,
Like her your movements are on legs of light steel.

Come and sit at my hearth, and I will celebrate your coming;

I will choose from the hundred flocks of each a hundred,
Passing at the foot of the Himalaya,

The two most silky and most beautiful great sheep.

We will go to the temple and sacrifice one of the two
To the god Pandu, that you may have many children;

And I will kill the other and roast it whole,

My most fair rose-tree serving as a spit.
I will ask the prettiest eaters and the prettiest drinkers;

And while they eat and drink greatly for three days,

I will wind silver rings upon your arms and feet
And hang a chain of river gold about your neck.

Popular Song of Kafiristan.

KAZACKS

YOU DO NOT WANT ME?

You do not want me, Zohrah.
Is it because I am maimed?
Yet
<u>Tamour-leng</u>
was maimed,
Going on crippled feet,
And he conquered the vast of the world.

You do not want me, Zohrah.

Is it because I am maimed?
Yet I have one arm to fight for you,
One arm to crush you to my rough breast,
One arm to break men for you.

It was to shield you from the Khargis

That I drag this stump in the long days.
It has been so with my women;
They would have made you a toy for heat.

After their chief with his axe once swinging

Cut my left arm, that, severed, bloody, and dead,
Yet struggled on the ground trying to guard you,
I have had pain for long in my arm that's lost.

Since the silk nets of your grape-lustrous eyes

Ensnared this heart that did not try to guard,

Ever I have a great pain in my heart that's lost.
You do not want me, Zohrah.

Kazack poem of the Chief Gahuan-Beyg (1850-1885).

KOREA

TEARS

How can a heart play any more with life,
  After it has found a woman and known tears?

In vain I shut my windows against the moonlight;
  I have estranged sleep.

The flower of her face is growing in the shadow
  Among warm and rustling leaves....

I see the sunlight on her house,
  I see her curtains of vermilion silk....

Here is the almond-coloured dawn;
  And there is dew on the petals of my night flower.

Lyric of Korea.

THE DREAM

I dreamed that I was touching her eyelids, and I awoke
To find her sleepy temples of rose jade
  For one heart-beat....

Though the moonlight beats upon the sea,
  There is no boat.

Lyric of Korea.

SEPARATION

As water runs in the river, so runs time;
And ever my eyes are wasted of her presence.

The red flowers of the second moon were yesterday;
To-day the earth has spots of blood, and there are no flowers.

The wild geese were harnessed to the autumn moon;
They have come, I heard their crying, and they are gone.
They have passed and given me no message;
I only hear the falling, falling noise of white rain.

Song of Korea.

KURDISTAN

PARADISE

Paradise, my darling, know that paradise,
The Prophet-given paradise after death,
Is far and very mysterious and most high;
My habits would be upset in such a place.

Without impiety, I should be mortally weary

If I went there alone, without my wife;
An ugly crowding of inferior females,
What should I do with the houris?

What should I do with those tall loaded fruit-trees,

Seeing I could not give the fruit to you?
What by the freshness of those blue streams,
Seeing my face reflected there alone?

And it might be worse if you came with me,

For all of Allah's Chosen would desire you.
And if Mahomet threw his handkerchief
And took you up and loved you for himself?

Eyes of my eyes, how could I then defend you?

I could not be at ease and watch him love you;
And if I mutinied against the Prophet,
He, being zealous to love you in his peace,

Would rise and send me hurrying

Back by the sword-blade thinness of the bridge

From paradise to earth, and in the middle
Flick me down sideways to the fires of hell.

My skin would cook and be renewed for ever

Where murderers were burning and renewing;
And evil souls, my only crime being love,
Would burn me and annoy me and destroy me.

If I were there and you in paradise,

I could not even make my prayer to Allah
That in his justice he should give me back
My paradise.

Let us love, therefore, on the earth together;

Our love is our garden, let us take great care,
Whisper and call pet names and kiss each other
To live our paradise as long as may be.

Love Ballad of Kurdistan.

LAOS

MISADVENTURE

Ever at the far side of the current
The fishes hurl and swim,
For pelicans and great birds
Watch and go fishing
On the bank-side.

No man dare go alone
In the dim great forest,
But if I were as strong
As the green tiger
I would go.

The holy swan on the sea
Wishes to pass over with his wings,
But I think it would be hard
To go so far.

If you are still pure,
Tell me, darling;
If you are no longer
Clear like an evening star,
You are the heart of a great tree
Eaten by insects.
Why do you lower your eyes?
Why do you not look at me?

When the blue elephant

Finds a lotus by the water-side
He takes it up and eats it.
Lemons are not sweeter than sugar.

If I had the moon at home

I would open my house wide
To the four winds of the horizon,
So that the clouds that surround her
Should escape and be shaken away.

Song of the Love Nights of Laos .

KHAP-SALUNG

Seeing that I adore you,
Scarf of golden flowers,
Why do you stay unmarried?
As the liana at a tree's foot
That quivers to wind it round,
So do I wait for you. I pray you
Do not detest me....

I have come to say farewell.

Farewell, scarf;
Garden Royal
Where none may enter,
Gaudy money
I may not spend.

Song of the Love Nights of Laos .

THE HOLY SWAN

Fair journey, O holy swan with gold wings;
O holy swan that I love, fair journey!
Carry this letter for me to the new land,

The place where my lover labours.
If it rains fly low beneath the trees,
If the sun is hot fly in the forest shadows;
If any ask you where you are going
Do not answer.
You who rise for so long a journey,
Avoid the roofs at the hour when the sun is red.
Carry this letter to the new land of my lover.
If he is faithful, give it to him;
If he has forgotten, read it to him only
And let the lightning burn it afterwards.

Song of the Love Nights of Laos .

MANCHURIA

FIRE AND LOVE

If you do not want your heart
Burnt at a small flame
Like a spitted sheep,
Fly the love of women.
Fire burns what it touches,
But love burns from afar.

Folk Song of Manchuria.

HEARTS OF WOMEN

It is hard for a man to tell
The hidden thought in his friend's heart,
And the thought in a man's own heart
Is a thing darker.

If you have seen a woman's heart

Bare to your eyes,
Go quickly away and never tell
What you have seen there.

Street Song of Manchuria.

PERSIA

TO HIS LOVE INSTEAD OF A PROMISED PICTURE-BOOK

The greater and the lesser ills:
  He waved his grey hand wearily
  Back to the anger of the sea,
Then forward to the blue of hills.

Out from the shattered barquenteen
  The black frieze-coated sailors bore
  Their dying despot to the shore
And wove a crazy palanquin.

They found a valley where the rain
  Had worn the fern-wood to a paste
  And tiny streams came down in haste
To eastward of the mountain chain.

And here was handiwork of Cretes,
  And olives grew beside a stone,
  And one slim phallos stood alone
Blasphemed at by the paroquets.

Hard by a wall of basalt bars
  The night came like a settling bird,
  And here he wept and slept and stirred
Faintly beneath the turning stars.

Then like a splash of saffron whey
  That spills from out a bogwood bowl

Oozed from the mountain clefts the whole
Rich and reluctant light of day.

And when he neither moved nor spoke

And did not heed the morning call,
They laid him underneath the wall
And wrapped him in a purple cloak.

From the Modern Persian.

TOO SHORT A NIGHT

Lily of Streams lay by my side last night
And to my prayers gave answers of delight;
Day came before our fairy-tale was finished,
Because the tale was long, not short the night.

From the Persian of Abu-Said (978-1062).

THE ROSES

Roses are a wandering scent from heaven.
Rose-seller, why do you sell your roses?
For silver? But with the silver from your roses
What can you buy so precious as your roses?

From the Persian of Abu-Yshac (middle of the tenth century).

I ASKED MY LOVE

I asked my love: "Why do you make yourself so beautiful?"
    «To please myself.
I am the eye, the mirror, and the loveliness;
The loved one and the lover and the love."

From the Persian of Abu-Said (978-1062).

A REQUEST

When I am cold and undesirous and my lids lie dead,
Come to watch by the body that loved you and say:
This is
Rondagui
, whom I killed and my heart regrets for ever.

From the Persian of Rondagui (tenth century).

SEE YOU HAVE DANCERS

See you have dancers and wine and a girl like one of the angels
    (If they exist),
And find a clear stream singing near its birth and a bed of moss
    (If moss exists),
For loving and singing to the dancers and drinking and forgetting hell
    (If hell exists),
Because this is a pastime better than paradise
    (If paradise exists).

From the Persian of Omar Khayyam (eleventh century).

SIAM

THE SIGHING HEART

> I made search for you all my life, and when I found you
> There came a trouble on me,
> So that it seemed my blood escaped
> And my life ran back from me
> And my heart slipped into you.
> It seems, also, that you are the moon
> And that I am at the top of a tree.
> If I had wings I would spread them as far as you,
> Dear bud, that will not open
> Though the kisses of the holy bird knock at your petal door.

Song of Siam.

SYRIA

HANDING OVER THE GUN

Kill me if you will not love me.
  Here are flints;
Ram down the heavy bullet, little leopard,
  On the black powder.

Only you must not shoot me through the head,
  Nor touch my heart;
Because my head is full of the ways of you
  And my heart is dead.

Song of Syria. ˙

TATARS

HONEY

Young man,
If you try to eat honey
On the blade of a knife,
You will cut yourself.

If you try to taste honey
On the kiss of a woman,
Taste with the lips only,
If not, young man,
You will bite your own heart.

Song of the Tatars.

THIBET

THE LOVE OF THE ARCHER PRINCE

The Khan.

The son of the Khan.

The love of the son of the Khan.

The veil of the love of the son of the Khan.

The clear breeze that lifted the veil of the love of the son of
the Khan.

The buds of fire that scented the clear breeze that lifted the
veil of the love of the son of the Khan.

The Archer Prince whose love kissed the buds of fire that
scented the clear breeze that lifted the veil of the love
of the son of the Khan.

And the girl married the Archer Prince whose love kissed the
buds of fire that scented the clear breeze that lifted the
veil of the love of the son of the Khan.

Street Song of Thibet.

TURKESTAN

DISTICH

Your face upon a drop of purple wine
Shows like my soul poised on a bead of blood.

From the Turkic of Hussein Baikrani.

THINGS SEEN IN A BATTLE

Clear diamond heart,
I have been hunting death
Among the swords.

But death abhors my shadow,
And I come back
Wounded with memories.

Your eyes,
For steel is amorous of steel
And there are bright blue sparks.

Your lips,
I see great bloody roses
Cut in white dead breasts.

Your bed,
For I see wrestling bodies
Under the evening star.

From the Turkic.

HUNTER'S SONG

Not a stone from my black sling
Ever misses anything,
But the arrows of your eye
Surer shoot and faster fly.

Not one creature that I hit

Lingers on to know of it,
But the game that falls to love
Lives and lingers long enough.

From the Turkic.

TURKEY

THE BATH

My dreams are bubbles of cool light,
Sunbeams mingled in the light green
Waters of your bath.

Through fretted spaces in the olive wood

My love adventures with the white sun.

I dive into the ice-coloured shadows

Where the water is like light blue flowers
Dancing on mirrors of silver.

The sun rolls under the waters of your bath

Like the body of a strong swimmer.

And now you cool your feet,

Which have the look of apple flowers,
Under the water on the oval marble
Coloured like yellow roses.

Your scarlet nipples

Waver under the green kisses of the water,
Flowers drowned in a mountain stream.

From the Modern Turkish.

DISTICH

Lions tremble at my claws;

And I at a gazelle with eyes.

From the Turkish of Sultan Selim I.

A PROVERB

Before you love,
Learn to run through snow
Leaving no footprint.

From the Turkish.

ENVOY IN AUTUMN

Here are the doleful rains,
And one would say the sky is weeping
The death of the tolerable weather.

Tedium cloaks the wit like a veil of clouds
And we sit down indoors.

Now is the time for poetry coloured with summer.

Let it fall on the white paper
As ripe flowers fall from a perfect tree.

I will dip down my lips into my cup
Each time I wet my brush.

And keep my thoughts from wandering as smoke wanders,

For time escapes away from you and me
Quicker than birds.

From the Chinese of Tu Fu (712-770).

TRANSLATOR'S NOTES

THE GARDEN OF BRIGHT WATERS

I am hoping that some readers will look on this collection primarily as a book of poems. The finding and selection of material and the shaping of the verses is my principal part in it. Most of the songs have been written from, or by comparing, the literal translations of French and Italian scholars, checked wherever possible by my own knowledge. When my first and very great debt to these has been stated, there remains my debt to the late John Duncan, to Mr. J. Wing, and to a friend, a distinguished writer both in Persian and Turkish, who wishes to remain unnamed. The kindness of these writers lies in trusting their work to my translation and helping me in that task. My book also owes much to suggestions prompted by the wide learning of Mr. L. Cranmer-Byng. My final debt is to him and to another generous critic. I have arranged my poems in the alphabetical order of their countries, and added short notes wherever I considered them necessary, at the instance of some kindly reviewers of an earlier book, which was not so arranged and provided.

AFGHANISTAN

SIKANDER, Alexander the Great.

SHALIBAGH, the notable garden of Shalimar in Lahore, planted by Shah Jahan in 1637.

ABDEL QADIR GILANI, Abd al-Qadir al-Jilani, founder of the Qadirite order of the Dervishes, twelfth century.

ANNAM

K'IEN NIÜ and CHIK NÜ: the legend of these two stars comes from China and is told in Japan. Readers are referred to that section of Mr. L. Cranmer-Byng's *A Lute of Jade* which deals delightfully with Po-Chü-i; and to Lafcadio Hearn›s *Romance of the Milky Way*.

ARABIC

ANTAR, the hero Antar Ebn Cheddad Ebn Amr Corad, who lived in the late sixth and early seventh centuries, owes his European reputation to *Siret Antar*, the Adventures of Antar, or more exactly the Conduct of Antar, written by Abul-Moyyed "El Antari" in the twelfth century. This book tells of the fighter's feats in war and of his love for his cousin Abla; and these are the themes of Antar's own poems.

AN ESCAPE: in this poem Abu Nuas, the Court poet, tells of an adventure of the Khalif Haroun. There is a story that the Khalif, being set back by the answer of his lady, called his poets in the morning and bade them write a poem round the phrase, "Words of a night to bring the day." All were rewarded for their work save Abu Nuas; and he was condemned to death for spying through keyholes on his master. But after he had proved an alibi, he also was rewarded.

"JOHN DUNCAN was a lowland Scot, who lived in Edinburgh until he was between twenty and twenty-five years old. He was educated at one of the Scots schools, and knew his way about the University if he was not actually a student there. He certainly had enough money to live on. A love affair in which he must have been infamously treated caused him to leave Scotland. Within a year or two he was an established member of a small tribe of nomadic Arabs, and eventually he became in speech and appearance one of them, living their lazy, pastoral life and travelling up and down with them the whole line of the southwest coast of the Persian Gulf. Before his death, which occurred last year, at the age of forty-two or forty-three, he had become acquainted with the whole of habitable Arabia.

"Let Mr. Mathers take up the story as he told it to me: 'He married an Arab, and all his forty-odd poems are addressed to her. I saw only a snapshot of her, which showed her to be beautiful. In her he certainly found healing for the wound his abnormally fiery and sensitive nature had taken from the first woman. She pulled together an intellect rather easily subdued. I only knew him after her death (his reason for travelling to this country), and a dazed, utterly unpractical and uninterested habit of mind, which alternated with his brilliance of speech and to a less degree of thought, was probably a reversion to the psychic state which his marriage had cured.

" 'Like so many to whom life has at one time given a paralysing shock, Duncan was extremely reticent, save when he could lead the conversation, and be confidential at points of his own choosing; and he was not an easy man to question. The disappointment which had driven him from his country certainly made him more bitter against the British than any other man I have listened to. All his considerable wit and the natural acid of his thought were directed against our ideas, institutions, and beliefs.

" 'His one sane enthusiasm, English lyric verse, of whose depths, mainstream, and back-waters his knowledge was profound, formed one-half of his conversation.

" 'His English in talking was rich and varied, and it was an ironic caprice which made him refuse to write in that language. I doubt, though, whether he would have composed with ease in any tongue, for he found it hard to concentrate, and his small stock of verse was the outcome of ten years of unoccupied life. He approved, rather mockingly, my promise to try to find an English equivalent for some of them; and I think I have copies of all he wrote.

" 'One not acquainted with the man might find them rather hard to render, as, had he been an Arab actually, still he would have been the most unconventional of poets, neglecting form and the literary language.'"

My most cordial thanks are due to The Bookworm, of the *Weekly Dispatch*, for permission to make this long quotation from an article headed, "The Strange Story of John Duncan, the Arab-Scot," which appeared over his *nom de plume* in the issue of that newspaper for March 30, 1919.

CHINA

J. WING: I have already translated three of this writer's poems: "English Girl," "Climbing after Nectarines," and "Being together at Night." These may be found in *Coloured Stars*. Mr. Wing is an American-born Chinese and practises the profession of a valet.

JAPAN

THE CLOCKS OF DEATH: this poem is a *zi-sei*, or lyric made at the point of death. Naga-Haru committed suicide after an unsuccessful defence of the strong castle Mi-Ki against Hashiba Hideyoshi in 1580. His wife followed his example, composing this poem as she died.

WAKANA, the turnip cabbage, whose leaves are eaten in early spring. The Mikado is lamenting a sudden realisation that he is too old for his love.

THE CUSHION: the poetess, daughter of Tsu-gu-naka, lord of Su-Wo, while at a party, asked for a cushion. A certain Iye-tada offered his arm for her to lean her head against, and she answered with these lines.

STREET SONGS: the three poems which I have so called are written in everyday colloquial Japanese. The words of the old language, which are the ornament of literary verse, are almost entirely excluded from these songs. In them one finds a superabundance of auxiliaries, and the presence of these marks a clear line between the literary and the folk-idiom.

KAZACKS

TAMOUR-LENG, Tamerlane. The facts of "You Do Not Want Me" are historical; but it should be added that Gahuan-Beyg succeeded in overcoming Zohrah's indifference, and that a few months after their marriage he beheaded her with his own hand for speaking to another man.

LAOS

THE LOVE NIGHTS OF LAOS, "Wan-Pak" Nights, at the eighth evening of the waxing or waning of the moon, when even Buddha has no fault to find with love-making in the thickets. Songs, of which I have translated three, are sung on these nights to the accompaniments of the "Khane," a pan-pipe of seven flutes; some being reserved for the singing of the wandering bands of girls, and others for answer by the youths.

PERSIA

THE ROSES, this rubai made Abu Yshac famous. He died at least twenty years before the birth of Omar Khayyam. Readers will have been struck by the similarity of idea in "The Roses" and in two lines in Fitzgerald's Rubaiyat:

I often wonder what the vintners buy
One-half so precious as the goods they sell.

THIBET

THE LOVE OF THE ARCHER PRINCE: this form of poem, with one rhyme and repetitive and increasing lines, is a familiar one in Thibet; and thence it has entered Kafiristan and become a popular manner of composition Archipelago. English readers will remember an analogous poem, "The House that Jack built."